BIOGRAPHIES

KAMALA HARRIS

by Jehan Jones-Radgowski

PEBBLE
a capstone imprint

Published by Pebble, an imprint of Capstone
1710 Roe Crest Drive, North Mankato, Minnesota 56003
capstonepub.com

Library of Congress Cataloging-in-Publication Data is available on the Library of Congress website
ISBN: 9781666350555 (hardcover)
ISBN: 9781666350722 (paperback)
ISBN: 9781666350685 (ebook PDF)

Summary: How much do you know about Vice President Kamala Harris? Discover the details you want to know about America's first female, Black, and Indian American vice president. You'll learn about Kamala's early life, challenges she overcame, and the accomplishments of this fierce politician.

Editorial Credits
Editor: Mandy Robbins; Designer: Hilary Wacholz; Media Researchers: Jo Miller and Deirdre Hiam; Production Specialist: Tori Abraham

Image Credits
Alamy: AF Archive, 25; Associated Press: George Nikitin, 7, Marcio Jose Sanchez, 15, 29, Rich Pedroncelli, 22, 23; Executive Office of the President of the United States/Lawrence Jackson, Cover, 1; Getty Images: Anadolu Agency, 27, Bettmann, 13, Jason Binn, 9; Newscom: ZUMA Press/Eric Slomanson, 18; Shutterstock: Biksu Tong, 5, Dallasetta, 11, eddie-hernandez.com, 19, Eric Glenn, 12, Featureflash Photo Agency, 21, Stephen Dorian Miner, 17

Printed and bound in the USA. PO4882

Table of Contents

Who Is Kamala Harris? 4

Growing Up Kamala 6

Making a Difference 10

A Working Momala 20

Kamala in the White House 26

Important Dates 28

Fast Facts 29

Glossary 30

Read More 31

Internet Sites 31

Index 32

About the Author 32

Words in **bold** are in the glossary.

Who Is Kamala Harris?

On January 20, 2021, Kamala Harris became the vice president of the United States. She raised her right hand proudly. She promised to support the United States.

Kamala is the first Black vice president. She is also the first female and first Indian American vice president. Her mother came to the United States from India. Her father came from Jamaica.

Growing Up Kamala

In 1958, Kamala's mother, Shyamala Gopalan, moved to America to study. Kamala's father, Donald Harris, moved there in 1961. They met at school in 1962. They married in 1963.

Kamala was born on October 20, 1964. She has a younger sister named Maya. They are best friends.

Kamala's mother stood with her as she was sworn in as San Francisco's district attorney in 2004.

Kamala's parents divorced when she was seven. The girls stayed with their mother. She taught them the **Hindu** religion. She also sent them to a local **Baptist** church.

When Kamala was 12, her family moved to Canada. The change was difficult. California was sunny. Canada was snowy. Kamala went to a French school. She did not speak French.

Kamala and her sister, Maya

Making a Difference

Kamala did not give up in Canada. She made new friends. One friend was having a difficult time at home. Kamala let her move in with her family. She stayed until things were better for her friend at her own home.

Kamala decided to become a lawyer. They help people. Kamala wanted to make sure everyone was treated equally.

Westmount High School, Quebec, where Kamala spent her high school years

Kamala went to college at Howard University in Washington, D.C. She joined Alpha Kappa Alpha, Inc. (AKA). It is the oldest Black **sorority**. In the summer, she worked for **Senator** Alan Cranston of California.

Howard University

Kamala went to law school at the University of California. She became a lawyer in 1989.

Kamala was a **prosecutor**. They make sure people who commit crimes are **punished**.

Kamala worked in a court. She faced off against other lawyers. In some cases, a judge decided who was right. In others, a group of people called a jury did that. Kamala showed them the facts. She tried to help them make the right call.

In 2003, Kamala ran for **district attorney**, or DA. The DA punishes companies and people who commit crimes in their area.

Kamala talked to many people to get their vote. She won! Kamala was San Francisco's first Black DA. She was the first Indian American and woman too.

Kamala and her team celebrate her election win.

As DA, Kamala helped people. Some had been waiting a long time for justice.

Others were former criminals. Kamala started programs to help them live better lives.

Kamala talking to reporters

Kamala and Doug Emhoff ride in San Francisco's Pride Parade in 2016.

In 2010, Kamala ran for attorney general. She won! She became the top lawyer for California.

A Working Momala

In 2014, Kamala married Doug Emhoff. He was a lawyer too. Doug had two children, Cole and Ella. Cole and Ella didn't want to call Kamala their stepmother. They called her "Momala." Kamala loves Cole and Ella. They enjoy family dinners on Sundays.

Kamala was busy with her new family. She was also busy as attorney general. She helped people who were losing their homes. Kamala stopped the company that was trying to make people move.

Kamala also helped foster kids. She made sure schools gave them extra help.

In 2016, Kamala ran for the U.S. Senate. Senators represent their state. There are only two for every state. She won! Kamala became a California senator.

As a senator, Kamala worked to help people be treated fairly. Kamala also helped immigrants. They are people who move to one country from another country. Kamala's parents were immigrants.

Kamala in the White House

In 2020, Kamala ran for president! She eventually dropped out, but Joe Biden didn't. In August 2020, he asked Kamala to run as his vice president.

On November 3, 2020, millions voted. Joe and Kamala won! Kamala became vice president of the United States.

Vice President Kamala Harris addresses a crowd alongside President Joe Biden.

Important Dates

1964	Kamala is born.
1976	Kamala moves to Canada.
1986	Kamala graduates from Howard University.
1989	Kamala graduates from University of California, Hastings College of the Law.
2004	Kamala becomes district attorney of San Francisco.
2011	Kamala becomes attorney general of California.
2014	Kamala marries Doug Emhoff.
2017	Kamala becomes a California representative in the U.S. Senate.
2019	Kamala publishes the children's book, *Superheroes Are Everywhere*.
2020	Joe Biden announces Kamala is his choice for vice president.
2021	Kamala is sworn in as vice president of the United States.

Fast Facts

Name:
Kamala Harris

Role:
vice president of the United States

Life dates:
Born 1964

Key accomplishments:
Kamala Harris has been San Francisco's district attorney, California's attorney general, a California senator, and vice president of the United States. She is also an author of three books.

Glossary

Baptist (BAP-tist)—a type of Christianity in which members must be old enough to state their beliefs to be baptized

district attorney (DIS-trikt uh-TER-nee)—a lawyer who is in charge of the cases against people accused of crimes

Hindu (HIN-doo)—a person who practices the religion of Hinduism; Hindus believe that they must live in harmony with universal laws

prosecutor (PROSS-uh-kew-tuhr)—a lawyer who represents the government in a criminal trial

punish (PUN-ish)—to make a person suffer for something he or she did wrong

senator (SEN-ah-tur)—a person elected to represent the people in the government; senators serve in the U.S. Senate

sorority (suh-ROR-uh-tee)—a society or club of women, especially in a college

Read More

Anderson, Kirsten. *Who Is Kamala Harris?* New York: Penguin Workshop, 2021.

Grimes, Nikki. *Kamala Harris: Rooted in Justice.* New York: Atheneum Books for Young Readers, 2020.

Harris, Kamala. *Superheroes Are Everywhere.* New York: Philomel Books, 2019.

Internet Sites

10 Things You May Not Know About Kamala Harris
biography.com/news/kamala-harris-facts

Kamala Harris
kids.britannica.com/kids/article/Kamala-Harris/631669

The White House: Kamala Harris, the Vice President
whitehouse.gov/administration/vice-president-harris/

Index

as a lawyer, 10, 13, 14, 19, 20
as a senator, 24, 28, 29
as attorney general, 19, 22, 28, 29
as district attorney, 7, 16, 18, 28, 29
as vice president, 4, 26, 27, 28, 29

Biden, Joe, 26, 27, 28
birth, 6, 28

Canada, 8, 10, 11, 28
Cranston, Alan, 12, 13

Emhoff, Cole, 20
Emhoff, Doug, 19, 20, 28
Emhoff, Ella, 20

Harris, Donald, 4, 6, 8, 24
Harris, Maya, 6, 8
Harris, Shyamala Gopalan, 4, 6, 7, 8, 24
Howard University, 12, 28

San Francisco, 7, 16, 19, 29

University of California, 13, 28

About the Author

Jehan Jones-Radgowski is the author of seven children's books. She received a bachelor's degree from George Mason University and an M.A. from George Washington University. She is also a U.S. Foreign Service Officer. She has lived with her three kids, husband, and dog worldwide, including the Dominican Republic, Germany, South Africa, Spain, the Russian Federation, the United States, and Venezuela. Jehan is also a member of Alpha Kappa Alpha, Inc. like Vice President Harris!